15 Fun-to-Sing

Math Learning Songs & Activities

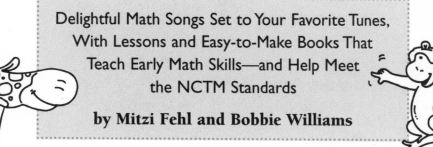

Delightful Math Songs Set to Your Favorite Tunes,
With Lessons and Easy-to-Make Books That
Teach Early Math Skills—and Help Meet
the NCTM Standards

by Mitzi Fehl and Bobbie Williams

SCHOLASTIC
PROFESSIONAL **B**OOKS

New York • Toronto • London • Auckland • Sydney
Mexico City • New Delhi • Hong Kong • Buenos Aires

·⊙· Dedication ⊙·

* To my K–1 class at Brookwood Elementary School for sharing their love of learning.

* And to my dearest friend and partner, Mitzi, for her creative talents in this project.

—Bobbie

* To my husband, Matthew; our girls, Mabree and Madison; and to my parents, Ray and Jo Humphries: thank you for your loving support and for believing in me.

* And to my dear friend and colleague, BW, for being my role-model in educating young children.

—Mitzi

Acknowledgments

* Ruth Chambers for taking pictures of our children.

* The children in my 1999–2000 K–1 Multiage Class for their work and enthusiasm.

* Emily Williams for her patience and endurance throughout the writing of this book.

—Bobbie

* Matthew Fehl for his guidance, honesty, and photography assistance.

* Mabree and Madison Fehl for making me laugh and keeping me on my toes.

* Penny Humphries, Charlene Hinshaw, Jane Jones, and Jodi King for the encouragement and shared excitement of this book.

* Martha Fehl for the advice along the way.

* Children of Poquoson Primary School for sharing your work and learning experiences, especially: Daniel, Elizabeth, Galen, Hannah, Jacob, Jessica, Joseph, Lily, Mark, Spencer, and William.

—Mitzi

Cover art by Steve Haskamp

Cover design by Josué Castilleja

Interior art by Rusty Fletcher

Interior design by Sydney Wright

ISBN: 0-439-18724-9
Copyright © 2002 by Mitzi Fehl and Bobbie Williams
All rights reserved.
Printed in the U.S.A.

Contents

Welcome!

"Twinkle, Twinkle Little Star."
"Row, Row, Row Your Boat."
"This Old Man." Familiar
tunes like these have delighted
children for generations.
Now you can make
them part of your math
curriculum with the easy
and fun lessons and collaborative books you'll find in these pages! We've changed
the words to these songs to create math lessons that actively involve children in
the learning process. With "Frogs on a Log," children will create addition-related
number sentences. With "Shape Town," children will experience shapes and
patterns. In each lesson, you and your class will be experiencing math by singing,
creating class big books, role-playing, using manipulatives, and more—all while
exploring popular classroom themes such as shapes, oceans, animals, and weather.

We hope that the combination of music, math, and language arts will enhance
your teaching and stimulate children's learning as they enjoy these lessons!

—Mitzi Fehl and Bobbie Williams

WHAT'S INSIDE

Each of the 15 lessons in this book enables you and your class to:

* experience a song together
* make a book
* extend and enrich learning beyond the lesson

Each section includes a reproducible song, a step-by-step Singing the Song activity
and Making the Book activity, materials lists, reproducible patterns, assessment tips,
cross-curricular activities, and related reading.

Reproducible Songs

Copy each song onto chart paper (you might laminate the chart paper so that you can use write-on/wipe-off markers to fill in the blanks, or simply write on self-sticking notes and place them in the designated blanks).

For shorter songs, you might write out the words on sentence strips to use with pocket charts.

Reproducible song pages can be copied and distributed to each child to read and color.

Snow Is Falling
(sing to "My Darlin' Clementine")

Snow is falling, snow is falling.
There stood ____ men of snow.
_____ built ____ to join them.
How many are in a row?

SINGING THE SONGS & MAKING THE BOOKS

Step-by-step instructions show you how to sing the song with the group and make the collaborative book.

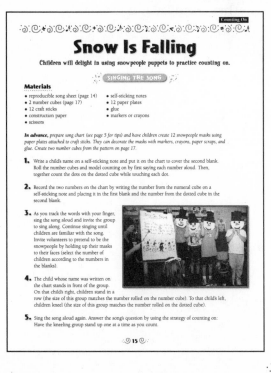

Singing the Songs

Sing the song once by yourself, tracking the words with your finger or a pointer as the group watches. On the second singing, invite children to join in. Repeat until all children are comfortable with the words and the melody.

Some lessons include a list of suggested props to be used. Children enjoy role-playing while singing the songs (this helps provide concrete understanding of the math concept).

Making the Books

Most of the books are collaborative books in which each child creates a page and all pages can then be bound into a class book.

Before children make their book page, explain the importance of not writing, drawing, or gluing on the left edge of the paper. This allows their work to be seen once the book is bound.

Children can design and decorate the covers of the books. You might laminate each page of the book for durability, or simply laminate the front and back cover.

There are many ways to compile and bind these big books. The type of binding used depends on the size and the number of pages. You might:

* Use a large metal ring.

* Use a binding machine for either the top or the side.

* Lace with ribbon or pipe cleaners.

* Staple the left edge.

* Use a three-hole punch and place in a binder.

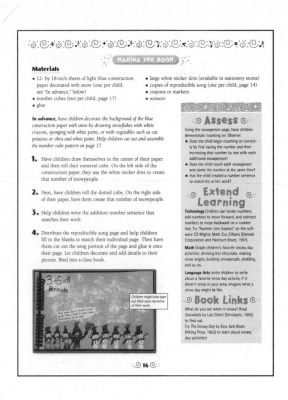

USING COLLABORATIVE BOOKS IN THE CLASSROOM

The collaborative books can enhance your classroom and curriculum in many ways:

* Add them to the library corner or math center.

* Display the book pages on a bulletin board before compiling them into a book.

* Invite children to take home the books nightly to read with their families. Children enjoy sharing these books at home, and this provides a fun home-school connection.

* If you have access to a computer, children can type their own story about the page they create or simply retype the song. They can cut out their story or song and glue it onto their book page.

* By the end of the year, you'll have a large collection of books made by your class. Instead of taking these apart so that children can each have their own work, allow every child to take home a book made by the class. Children are proud to share their work with others!

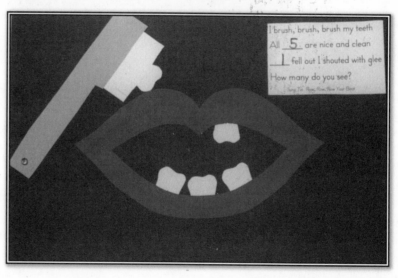

Connections to the NCTM Standards 2000

	Numbers and Operations	Estimation*	Number Sense and Numeration*	Concepts of Whole-Number Operations*	Whole-Number Computation*	Fractions and Decimals*	Patterns, Functions, and Algebra	Geometry and Spatial Sense	Measurement	Data Analysis, Statistics, and Probability	Problem Solving	Reasoning and Proof	Communication	Connections	Representation
How Many in the Jar?		•									•	•	•		•
Snow Is Falling			•							•	•		•		•
Oh, Mr. Postman				•	•						•		•		•
Frogs on a Log				•	•						•		•		•
Brush, Brush, Brush				•	•						•		•		•
Mama Monkey				•	•						•		•		•
Pizza Pieces						•					•		•		•
Houses All Around							•				•		•		•
The Mystery Box							•				•	•	•		•
Shape Town								•			•		•		•
The Zoo									•		•		•		•
Under the Sea									•		•		•		•
The Piggy Bank					•				•		•		•		•
To the Grocery Store										•	•		•	•	•
Ladybug Spots, Ladybug Dots			•								•		•		•

* Indicates a subcategory of Numbers and Operations

Learning Songs & Activities

How Many in the Jar?

(sing to "B-I-N-G-O")

There is a jar that's filled with _____

Oh, estimate the number!

How many do you see?

How many do you see?

How many do you see?

Go write it down and tell me!

How Many in the Jar?

Use this lesson all year long to help children develop estimation skills.

SINGING THE SONG

Materials

* reproducible song sheet (page 10)
* jar
* objects such as jelly beans, buttons, or beans

In advance, prepare song chart (see page 5 for tips).

1. Select an object to be used in the estimation jar, and fill the jar. (Use the same jar each time you do this lesson. The younger the class, the smaller the jar. For example, kindergarten classes might use a baby food jar, but a second-grade class might select a peanut butter jar.) Write the name of the object on the blank in your song chart.

2. With children in a circle, sing the song aloud as you track the words. Then invite children to sing along. As they do so, have them pass the jar around the circle and examine the objects in the jar. Continue singing the song until all children have had a turn holding and looking at the jar.

3. Invite children to estimate the number of objects in the jar and begin making their own estimate pages (see next page).

Materials

* copies of page 13 (one per child)
* pencils, crayons, markers

1. Have children record their estimate on the page and illustrate the contents of the jar (the number should reflect their estimate). Then have children bring their pages back to the circle.

2. With the class, count the number of objects in the estimation jar. (If the jar contains more than ten objects, use portion cups to count out groups of 10. When totaling the items, count out loud by tens with your children.)

3. On their page, have children record the correct number of objects and the name of the object in the jar. Encourage children to share their original estimate and discuss its relationship to the correct number of objects in the jar.

4. Bind all pages together into a class book.

Children might also create their own estimation journals.

Assess

Using children's individual estimate pages, observe:
* Does the child observe the contents of the jar and make an "informed guess"?
* Has the child created a drawing that matches his or her estimation?
* Can the child describe his or her estimation strategy?

Extend Learning

Home Connection Have children take turns filling the jar at home, using any item they choose. When they return to school with the filled jar, repeat this lesson.

Circle Time Ask children to signal with their hands the estimates they made. Have children make a thumbs-up if their guess was too high, thumbs-down if too low, or a fist if just right.

Book Links

The Button Box, by Margarette S. Reid (Dutton, 1990), explores the history of buttons.

Bruce McMillan's *Jelly Beans for Sale* (Scholastic, 1996) explores the concept of money and peaks curiosity about jelly beans. Includes the history of jelly beans and a recipe.

Counting on Frank by Rob Clement (Gareth Stevens, 1991) is a delightful and unique view of the world according to a boy who could claim to be the "king of estimating."

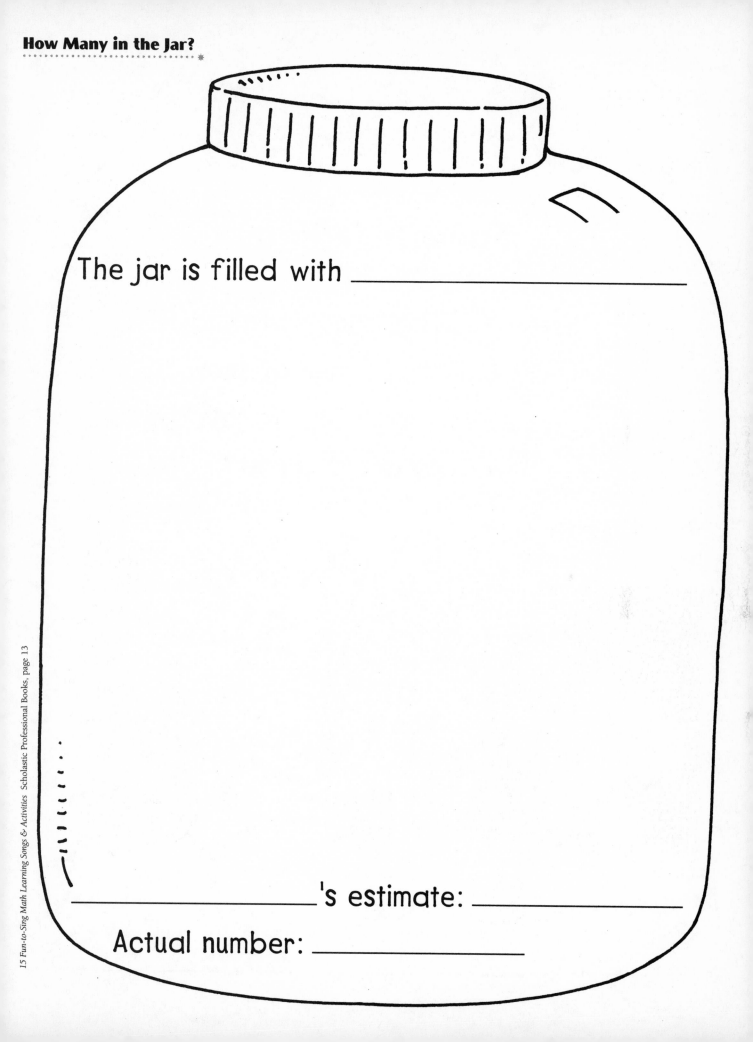

The jar is filled with _____

_____ 's estimate: _____

Actual number: _____

Snow Is Falling

(sing to "My Darlin' Clementine")

Snow is falling, snow is falling.

There stood _____ men of snow.

_____ built _____ to join them.

How many are in a row?

Snow Is Falling

Children will delight in using snowpeople puppets to practice counting on.

SINGING THE SONG

Materials

* reproducible song sheet (page 14)
* 2 number cubes (page 17)
* 12 craft sticks
* construction paper
* scissors
* self-sticking notes
* 12 paper plates
* glue
* markers or crayons

In advance, prepare song chart (see page 5 for tips) and have children create 12 snowpeople masks using paper plates attached to craft sticks. They can decorate the masks with markers, crayons, paper scraps, and glue. Create two number cubes from the pattern on page 17.

1. Write a child's name on a self-sticking note and put it on the chart to cover the second blank. Roll the number cubes and model counting on by first saying each number aloud. Then, together count the dots on the dotted cube while touching each dot.

2. Record the two numbers on the chart by writing the number from the numeral cube on a self-sticking note and placing it in the first blank and the number from the dotted cube in the second blank.

3. As you track the words with your finger, sing the song aloud and invite the group to sing along. Continue singing until children are familiar with the song. Invite volunteers to pretend to be the snowpeople by holding up their masks to their faces (select the number of children according to the numbers in the blanks).

4. The child whose name was written on the chart stands in front of the group. On that child's right, children stand in a row (the size of this group matches the number rolled on the number cube). To that child's left, children kneel (the size of this group matches the number rolled on the dotted cube).

5. Sing the song aloud again. Answer the song's question by using the strategy of counting on: Have the kneeling group stand up one at a time as you count.

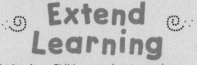
Materials

* 12- by 18-inch sheets of light blue construction paper decorated with snow (one per child, see "In advance," below)
* number cubes (two per child, page 17)
* glue

* large white sticker dots (available in stationery stores)
* copies of reproducible song (one per child, page 14)
* crayons or markers
* scissors

In advance, have children decorate the background of the blue construction paper with snow by drawing snowflakes with white crayons, sponging with white paint, or with vegetables such as cut potatoes or okra and white paint. Help children cut out and assemble the number cube pattern on page 17.

1. Have children draw themselves in the center of their paper and then roll their numeral cube. On the left side of the construction paper, they use the white sticker dots to create that number of snowpeople.

2. Next, have children roll the dotted cube. On the right side of their paper, have them create that number of snowpeople.

3. Help children write the addition number sentence that matches their work.

4. Distribute the reproducible song page and help children fill in the blanks to match their individual page. Then have them cut out the song portion of the page and glue it onto their page. Let children decorate and add details to their picture. Bind into a class book.

3+5=8

Brooke

One snow day I built 3 snow girls. Then I built 5 snow men. How many in a row?

Children might also type out their own narrative of their work.

Assess

Using the snowperson page, have children demonstrate counting on. Observe:

* Does the child begin counting on correctly by first saying the number and then increasing that number by one with each additional snowperson?
* Does the child touch each snowperson and name the number at the same time?
* Has the child created a number sentence to match his or her work?

Extend Learning

Technology Children can locate numbers, add numbers to move forward, and subtract numbers to move backward on a number line. Try "Number Line Express" on the software CD Mighty Math Zoo Zillions (Edmark Corporation and Harcourt Brace, 1997).

Math Graph children's favorite snowy day activities: drinking hot chocolate, making snow angels, building snowpeople, sledding, and so on.

Language Arts Invite children to write about a favorite snow day activity. If it doesn't snow in your area, imagine what a snow day might be like.

Book Links

What do you see when it snows? Read *Snowballs* by Lois Ehlert (Scholastic, 1995) to find out.

Try *The Snowy Day* by Ezra Jack Keats (Viking Press, 1962) to learn about snowy day activities!

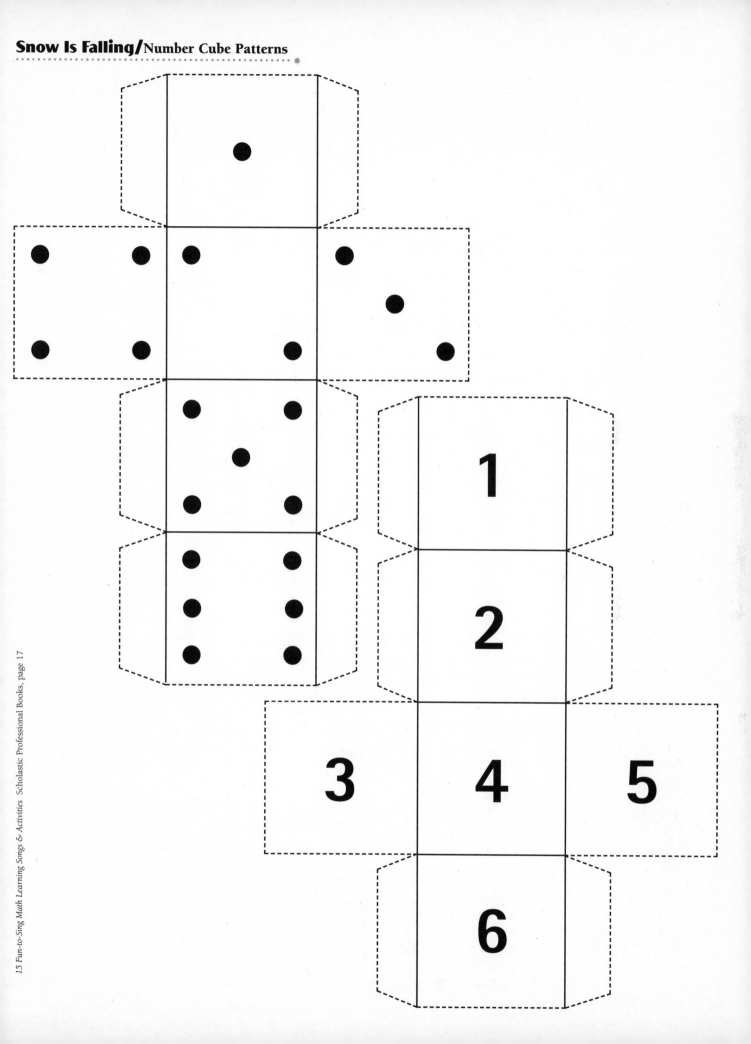

Oh, Mr. Postman

(sing to "Oh, Susanna")

Oh, Mr. Postman,

Now whatcha got for me?

I have _____ letters,

I'd like _____ more.

How many would that be?

Oh, Mr. Postman

Children will be eager to fill their very own mailboxes to create number sentences.

SINGING THE SONG

Materials

* reproducible song sheet (page 18)
* self-sticking notes
* bookbag or backpack

* hat
* 10 or more envelopes
* marker

In advance, prepare song chart (see page 5 for tips).

1. Sing aloud as you track the words. Then sing again, inviting children to join in. Continue until children are familiar with the song. Model how to fill in the number blanks on the chart with self-sticking notes to make different number combinations.

2. Invite two children to use the mail props to act out the song (one child is the postman and the other the receiver of the mail) using the number of "letters" indicated.

3. Write the matching number sentence on the bottom of the chart (for instance, 3 + 5 = 8). Repeat several times, using different number combinations in the blanks.

Materials

- 12- by 18-inch construction paper
- envelope and mailbox patterns
  (one per child, pages 21–22, page 22 can
  be copied onto colored construction paper)
- reproducible song sheet
  (one per child, page 18)
- glue
- scissors
- brad fasteners
- single hole punch
- 6- to 8-inch pieces of yarn (one per child)
- tape
- crayons or markers

1. Have children cut out and glue the mailbox post to the bottom left corner of the construction paper. Then have them cut out the mailbox flag and attach it to the mailbox pattern with a brad. Then have them glue the mailbox pattern onto the construction paper, leaving the right edge of the pattern without glue to make a side pocket.

2. Children decide on the total number of letters they want to use. Have them glue some of those letters onto the construction paper to represent the number of letters they've already received.

3. Help children punch holes in the other letters and thread yarn through the holes. Tape down both ends of the yarn underneath the open end of the mailbox. These letters represent how many more letters children would like to receive from the postman! You should be able to pull them in and out of the mailbox.

4. Children write their name and the number sentence that matches their work on the page. (Children might also write the number of their own residence on the mailbox.)

5. Distribute the reproducible song to each child, and have children record their numbers in the correct blanks, cut out the song, and glue it onto their individual page. Bind all pages together into a class book.

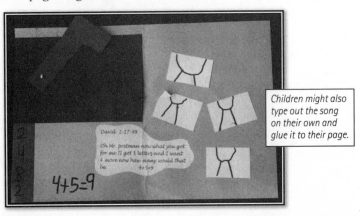

Children might also type out the song on their own and glue it to their page.

Assess

On each child's individual book page, notice the following:
- Is the problem solved accurately?
- Was the child able to write a number sentence that correctly matches his or her work?
- Can the child tell a story that represents his or her work?

Extend Learning

Language Arts Set up a post office in the classroom. Invite children to write messages to their friends. Then have children take turns being the postman, delivering the letters to children.

Social Studies Arrange a trip to the local post office.

Book Links

Visit with your favorite nursery rhyme characters in *The Jolly Postman*, by Janet and Allan Ahlberg (Little Brown, 1986), as the postman delivers letters to each one.

Sing along as you read *Mail Myself to You*, by Woody Guthrie (Good Year, 1994), which is about wrapping yourself up and mailing yourself to a friend!

Oh, Mr. Postman

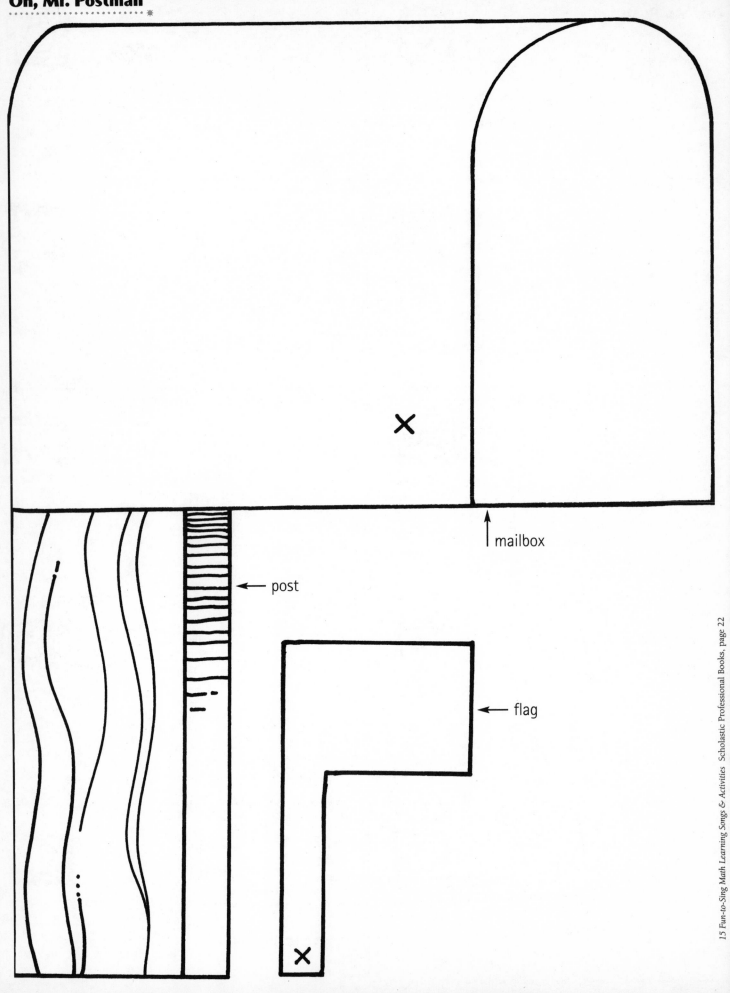

post

mailbox

flag

Frogs on a Log

(sing to "This Old Man")

_____ green frogs

Sitting on a log

They croaked all night through the fog

'Til _____ more came and joined their little song.

Now there are _____ getting along.

Frogs on a Log

Children manipulate frog puppets to create addition number sentences.

SINGING THE SONG

Materials

* reproducible song sheet (page 23)
* 13 self-sticking notes numbered 0–12
* egg carton (painted brown)
* frog craft stick puppets (one per child, page 26, copied onto green construction paper)
* frog headbands (one per child, page 27)

In advance, prepare song chart (see page 5 for tips). Then, turn the egg carton upside down and cut slits in the egg holders for the frog puppets to slide into. Attach frog reproducibles to craft sticks. Have children create frog headbands by coloring the pattern and attaching it to a strip of oaktag sized to fit their head.

1. Sing aloud as you track the words. Then sing again, inviting children to join in. Continue until children are familiar with the song.

2. Using the egg carton as the log and the frog stick puppets, act out the numbers in the song. Repeat, changing the number combinations (put the self-sticking notes on the blanks in the chart) to reinforce the addition concept.

3. Model how to write an addition number sentence to match the number of frogs on the log. Ask volunteers to come forward and manipulate the frogs as the class sings the song. Children can then act out the song themselves with their frog headbands.

Materials

* 12- by 18-inch sheets of white construction paper
* reproducible song sheet (page 23)
* frog reproducibles (one sheet per child, page 26)
* markers or crayons

1. Have children fold the construction paper to make a flap about one third of the way across as indicated. Then have them open the construction paper to draw the background and a log. Then have them fold the paper again and continue drawing the length of the log as well as additional background on the flap. (Be sure the flap is folded before children glue their frogs on the log. Encourage children to put some frogs on the log drawn on the flap as well. This prevents the frogs from being hidden behind the flap.)

2. Have children cut out and glue the reproducible song onto their page and fill in the correct numbers according to their drawing. The first number is the number of frogs seen when the construction paper is opened up; the second number is the number of frogs drawn only on the flap; and the final number is the total number of frogs seen when the paper is folded.

3. Help children write a number sentence to match their work. Bind all pages together into a class book.

Assess

Look at children's pages to assess the following:
* Did the child solve the problem independently?
* Is the problem solved accurately?
* Was the child able to correctly write a number sentence to reflect his or her work?
* Can the child tell a story that represents his or her work?

Extend Learning

Language Arts Read frog and toad books and create a Venn diagram comparing and contrasting the two animals.

Science and Technology Study the life cycle of the frog and use a computer drawing program to illustrate the stages of growth.

Book Links

Frog on a Log, by Norma L. Genter (Wright, 1995), is a book of frog facts set to a catchy tune.

Jump into Robert Kalan's *Jump Frog Jump* (Mulberry, 1981), as the frog leaps from place to place seeking safety.

Brush, Brush, Brush

(sing to "Row, Row, Row Your Boat")

I brush, brush, brush my teeth

All _____ are nice and clean

_____ fell out, I shouted with glee!

How many do you see?

Brush, Brush, Brush

Children will enjoy singing about losing their teeth
and learning about subtraction at the same time.

SINGING THE SONG

Materials

* reproducible song sheet (page 28)
* self-sticking notes
* toothbrush

*In advance, prepare song sheet
(see page 5 for tips).*

1. Sing the song aloud and invite children to sing along. Continue until children are familiar with the song.

2. Model how to fill in the number blanks with self-sticking notes to make different number combinations. Then invite children to use the toothbrush to act out the song.

3. Sing the song, using different number combinations written on the large chart.

4. Demonstrate how to write a matching number sentence at the bottom of the chart.

You can also create large props with colored posterboard.

Materials

- 12- by 18-inch sheets of black construction paper
- mouth, tooth, and toothbrush pattern (one per child, page 31)
- glue
- reproducible song sheet (one per child, page 28)
- scissors
- brad fasteners
- crayons or markers
- white crayon

1. Have children color, cut out, and glue the mouth pattern onto their construction paper. They can then color and cut out the toothbrush shape (to make the brush appear real, cut the bristles on the pattern) and attach it to their page with a brad.

2. Have children cut out the total number of teeth they want on their page. Children can then glue to the bristle end of the toothbrush the number of teeth they want to fall out. The other teeth are placed under the edge of the lips on both the top and bottom of the mouth.

3. Children write their number sentence in white crayon on the black paper. They can cut out and glue the song onto their page and fill in the correct numbers.

4. Bind all pages together into a book.

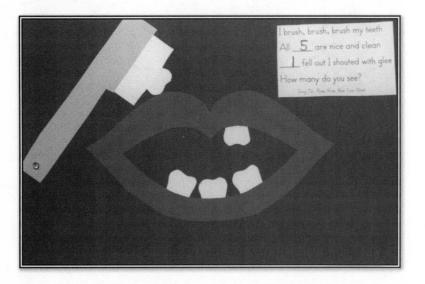

Assess

Viewing the child's individual book page, check the following:
- Did the child solve the problem independently?
- Is the problem solved accurately?
- Was the child able to write a number sentence that correctly matches his or her work?
- Can the child tell a story that represents his or her work?

Extend Learning

Math Make a lost tooth graph to use all year long so that children can see how many teeth are lost each month by their class.

Social Studies/Health Visit a dentist's office, or have a dental hygienist visit to talk about dental health.

Book Links

Throw Your Tooth on the Roof, by Selby B. Beeler (Houghton Mifflin, 1998). Journey around the world learning about tooth traditions of young children.

Remember the anticipation of losing your first tooth in *The Lost Tooth Club,* by Arden Johnson (Tricycle Press, 1998).

In *A Wiggly, Jiggly, Joggly Tooth,* by Bill Hawley (Good Year, 1994), readers will shout with glee at the surprise ending.

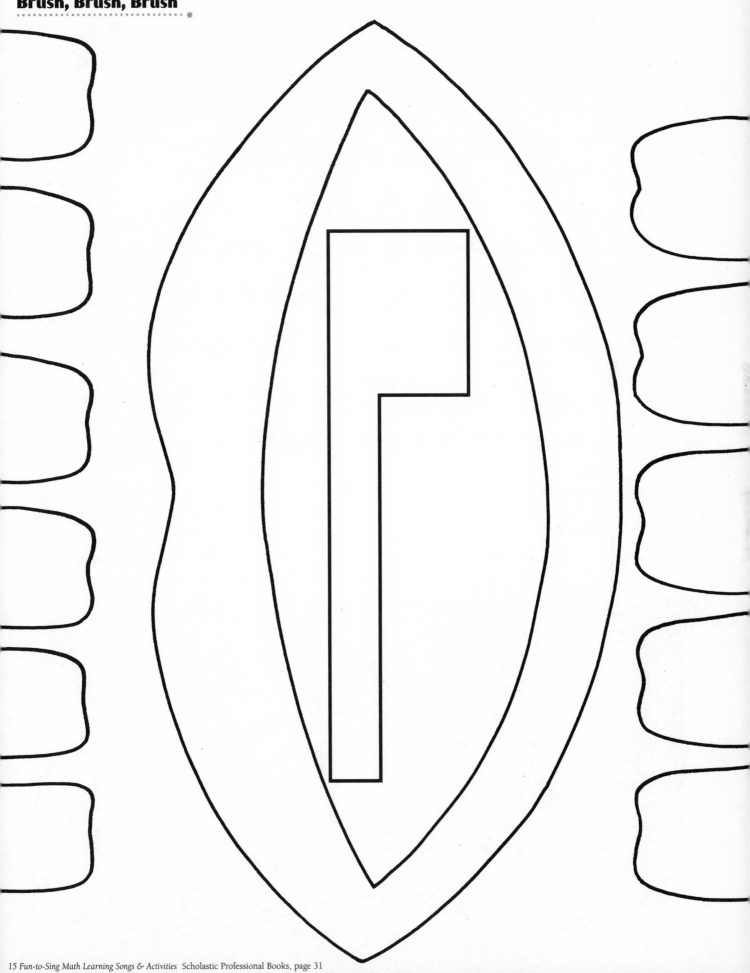

Mama Monkey

(sing to "This Old Man")

Oh mama monkey, heard some noise.

It came from her girls and boys.

She watched all _____ swinging in the trees

_____ climbed down.

Who's left to see?

Mama Monkey

Children "monkey around" with subtraction!

SINGING THE SONG

Materials

* reproducible song sheet (page 32)
* monkey headbands (one per child, page 35, copied onto brown construction paper)
* self-sticking notes

In advance, prepare song chart (see page 5 for tips) and use oaktag strips to create monkey headbands, then tape the ends of the headbands together.

1. Sing aloud as you track the print. Then sing again, inviting children to join in. Continue singing until children are familiar with the song.

2. Show children how to fill in the number blanks (using self-sticking notes) to make different number combinations on the large song sheet.

3. Invite volunteers to wear their monkey headbands and act out the song, using the number combinations written on the chart.

4. Demonstrate how to write a number sentence that corresponds with the role-play and the numbers on the chart. Repeat, substituting different number combinations and encouraging other children to participate.

MAKING THE BOOK

Materials

* reproducible song sheet (page 32)
* 12- by 18-inch white construction paper (folded as shown below)
* water
* brown and green tempera paint
* sponge
* crayons or markers

1. Model for children how to position their paper vertically and then make a fold about one third of the way up their paper.

2. Then direct them to unfold the flap and create a tree with limbs and color using the sponge and paint. The tree should extend the entire length of their page.

3. When the paper is dry, demonstrate how to refold the flap and recreate the lower part of the tree on the outside of the flap. It should look just like the bottom of the tree they made inside.

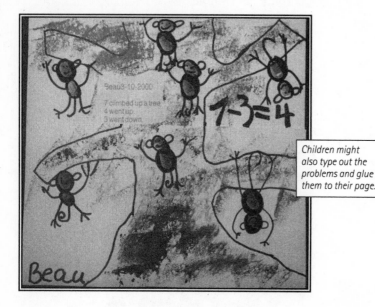

Children might also type out the problems and glue them to their page.

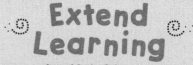

☺ Assess ☺

While viewing the student page, check the following:

* Did the child solve the problem independently?
* Is the problem solved accurately?
* Was the child able to correctly write a number sentence to match his or her work?
* Can the child tell a story that represents his or her work?

Extend Learning

Language Arts, Math, Science, and Social Studies Read about monkeys and focus on four or five different types. Try the following activities with the information that you discover:

* Have children vote on their favorite monkey and graph results.
* Use a map to locate where the monkeys live.
* Create a Venn diagram comparing and contrasting two different types of monkeys.
* Illustrate the habitats of each monkey.

☺ Book Links ☺

Explore counting backward in *Five Little Monkeys*, by Eileen Christelow (Clarion, 1991), as five monkeys discover why it's unwise to tease a crocodile.

Monkeys in the Jungle, by Angie Sage (Houghton Mifflin, 1991), is a fun-filled book of rhymes that will delight readers as they count the animals at the end.

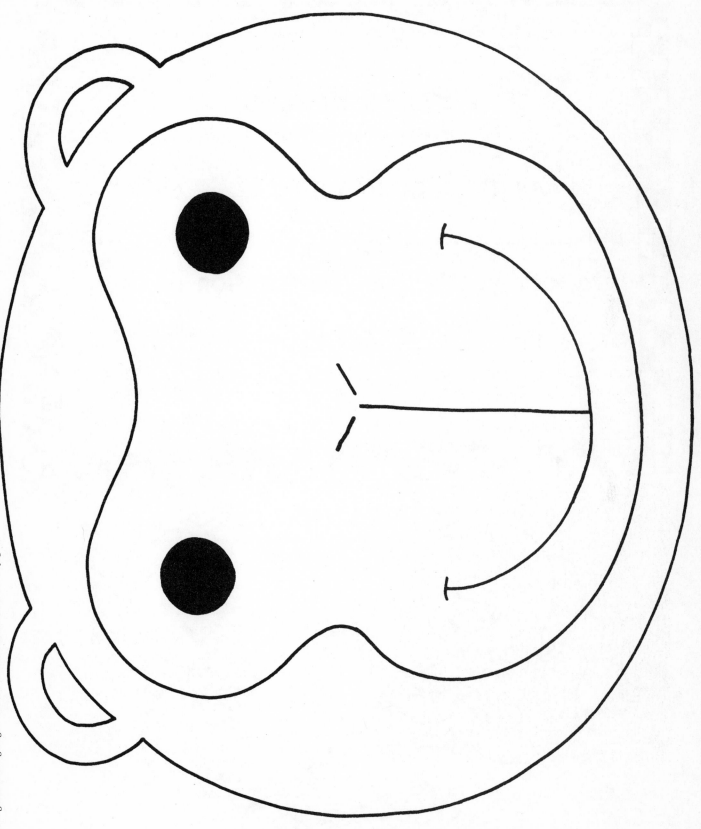

Pizza Pieces

(sing to "You Are My Sunshine")

I bought a pizza with _____ slices.

But _____ ate _____ before I did.

Oh, can you tell me the fraction of pizza

that is under the pizza box lid?

Pizza Pieces

Make fractions fun and easy with this delicious topic!

SINGING THE SONG

Materials

* reproducible song sheet (page 36)
* self-sticking notes
* large pretend pizza

In advance, prepare song chart (see page 5 for tips).

1. Begin with a "pizza" cut into four equal pieces. Sing aloud as you track the print. Then sing again, inviting children to join in. Continue singing until children are familiar with the song.

2. Sing the song again, using a child's name in the blank (use self-sticking notes for the names and numbers). That child can participate by pretending to eat the number of pieces you sing about. Then encourage children to answer the question at the end of the song.

3. Repeat this activity, varying the number of pieces and modeling how to write the fractions for each.

Pretend pizza is available in teacher supply stores, or you can create your own with poster board, markers, paper, and a used pizza box.

MAKING THE BOOK

Materials

- 12- by 18-inch brown construction paper
- paper plates
- reproducible song sheet (one per child, page 36)
- scrap paper for creating "ingredients"

- answer page (one per child, page 39)
- glue
- scissors
- crayons or markers

1. Have children color and decorate their paper plate with crayons and markers, gluing on the paper scraps for ingredients. When dry, they can cut the plate into equal slices.

2. Have children fold the brown construction paper in half from top to bottom (the flap is the pizza box lid). Open the box and glue a certain number of slices of pizza inside.

3. Help children fill in the blanks on the reproducible song sheet, cut it out, and attach the song to the inside of the lid. They can then fill out their answer page and glue it next to the song.

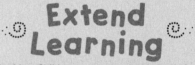

Assess

Gather children in small groups with the pizza props. Make observations while asking the following questions:

- If the pizza is cut into four equal pieces and I give you one, how many are left?
- What is the fraction of pizza that was removed?
- Repeat, varying the number of slices.

Extend Learning

Cooking Children can create and bake their own pizzas with English muffins, pizza sauce, cheese, and Italian seasoning.

Drama Set out kitchen supplies, aprons, and so on, so that children can act out making pizza.

Book Links

Explore the concepts of fractions and money through rhyme and rhythm in *A Slice of Pizza*, by Marcie Bovetz (Wright, 1999).

Eating Fractions, by Bruce McMillan (Scholastic, 1991), uses photographs to discover fractional parts of foods. The author even shares his favorite recipes!

The fraction of pizza is:

Houses All Around

(sing to "This Old Man")

Houses all around

Through our town

Lots of colors can be found

From red, blue, white,

Yellow, black, and green.

What's the pattern that is seen?

Houses All Around

Children will have fun identifying and creating patterns.

SINGING THE SONG

Materials

* reproducible song sheet (page 40)
* flannel board
* felt house shapes (use colors from song)
* Unifix™ cubes in colors from the song

In advance, *prepare song chart (see page 5 for tips).*

1. Sing aloud as you track the words. Then sing again, inviting children to join in. Continue until children are familiar with the song.

2. Model how to create a color pattern using a flannel board and felt houses.

3. Distribute the Unifix™ cubes and invite children to copy the pattern displayed. Repeat this step until children demonstrate an understanding of this concept.

4. Sing the song again, and invite a child to create their own pattern for the class to copy. If time allows, have children work in pairs, singing the song while one child creates a pattern for the others to copy.

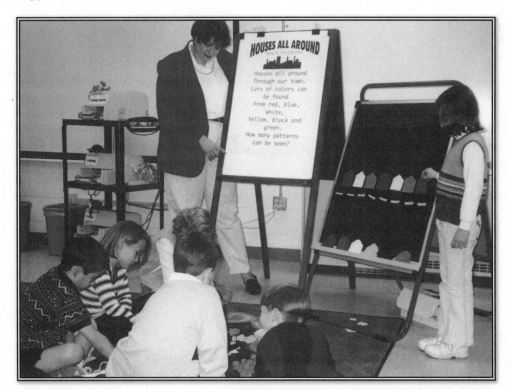

MAKING THE BOOK

Materials

* 12- by 18-inch construction paper (white or light blue)
* reproducible song sheet (one per child, page 40)
* house patterns (one sheet per child, page 43)
* glue
* scissors
* crayons or markers

1. Have children draw a line to create a "street" on their sheet of construction paper.

2. Invite children to color, cut out, and glue their houses in a pattern along their "street."

3. Have children cut out and glue the reproducible song onto their page.

4. Have children add details on their book page. Bind together into a class book.

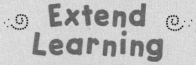

⊙ Assess ⊙

Using any manipulative, create an AB pattern and have each child reproduce and extend the pattern. Repeat this activity with other pattern formats such as ABB, AABB.

Go on a pattern walk and observe whether children can identify patterns in their environment.

Extend Learning

Technology Explore "Pattern Block Roundup" on the software CD Mighty Math Carnival Countdown (Edmark Corporation and Harcourt Brace, 1996), as children create designs, fill in patterns, and explore symmetry.

Math Have children create their own house with construction paper. Upon completion, organize these houses into a graph. Sort them by color, number of windows, and so on.

Social Studies In a center, place paper houses (you might simply use page 43) with each child's house or apartment number written on them. Provide addressed envelopes of each child's residence for children to match with the corresponding house.

⊙ Book Links ⊙

To learn about houses from around the world, young readers will enjoy the photographs in *Houses* by Ann Morris (Good Year, 1996).

To explore patterns in the environment, view photographs in *Patterns* by Henry Pluckrose (Childrens Press, 1995).

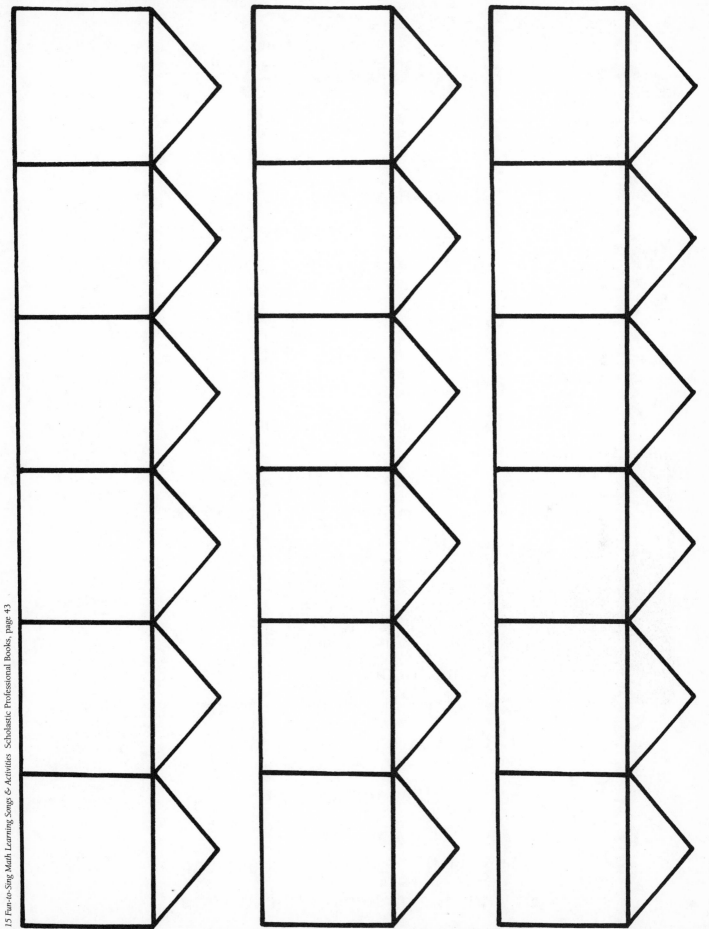

The Mystery Box

(sing to "Mary Had a Little Lamb")

_____ has a mystery box

Mystery box, mystery box

_____ has a mystery box

Oh, guess what makes that knock!

Can you guess the size of it?

Size of it, size of it?

Can you guess the size of it?

Big or small, what is the fit?

Any color...black, maybe blue.

Black maybe blue, black maybe blue.

Any color...black, maybe blue.

Now figure out this clue!

Rough or smooth to the touch

To the touch, to the touch?

Rough or smooth to the touch

Can you tell us that much?

Go sort the facts and figure out

Figure out, figure out.

Go sort the facts and figure out

Just what the mystery box is all about!

The Mystery Box

Children reflect upon attributes to solve a mystery.

SINGING THE SONG

Materials

* reproducible song sheet (page 44)
* large box decorated with question marks
* solid-color object to fit in the box (apple, rock, shell, ball, or any theme-related object)

1. Sing aloud as you track the words. Then sing again, inviting children to join in. Continue singing until children are familiar with the song.

2. Sing the song once again, stopping after each verse and encouraging children to reflect on the question. Discuss the attributes mentioned (color, size, texture, and so on). Children can ask yes-or-no questions as well.

3. Sing the last verse, and invite children to complete their page (see Making the Book).

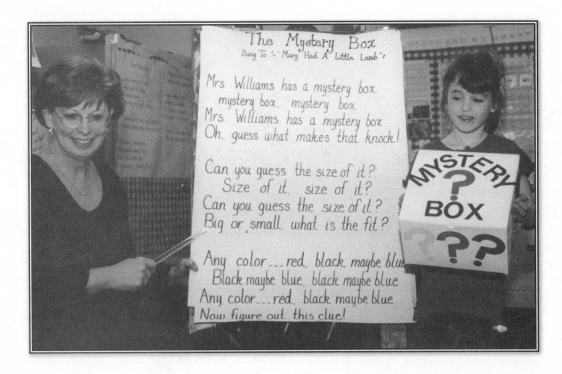

Materials

* recording sheet
  (one per child, page 47)
* crayons or markers
* pencils

1. Have children record what they think is in the box by drawing a picture and writing about it.

2. Encourage children to share their predictions, then open the mystery box to see the hidden item.

3. Bind all pages together into a book!

Assess

Look at the predictions of each child. *Did their guess fit the attributes that were discovered?* (For example, if the attributes of the object were orange in color, bumpy to the touch, and round in shape, the child might guess an orange rather than a basketball.)

Extend Learning

Home Connection Allow each child the opportunity to bring in from home an object for the mystery box, and repeat the activity using his or her name in the song.

Technology On the software CD Mighty Math Carnival Countdown (Edmark Corporation and Harcourt Brace, 1996), children can practice sorting cars into sets with the program "Carnival Cars."

Book Links

Read Tana Hoban's books *Is It Red? Is It Yellow? Is It Blue?* (Greenwillow, 1978), *Is It Larger? Is It Smaller?* (Greenwillow, 1985), and *Is It Rough? Is It Smooth? Is It Shiny?* (Greenwillow, 1984) to introduce children to color, size, and texture. Each book is a collection of photographs showing each attribute up close.

Name _____

What is in the box? I think it is a _____

because _____

_____

_____.

It was a _____.

Shape Town

(sing to "If You're Happy and You Know It")

There are shapes all around in our town.

There are shapes all around in our town.

There are shapes all around,

Take a look at what we found.

There are shapes all around in our town.

There are shapes all around in our town.

There are shapes all around in our town.

There are shapes all around,

Where's the _____ that we found?

There are shapes all around in our town.

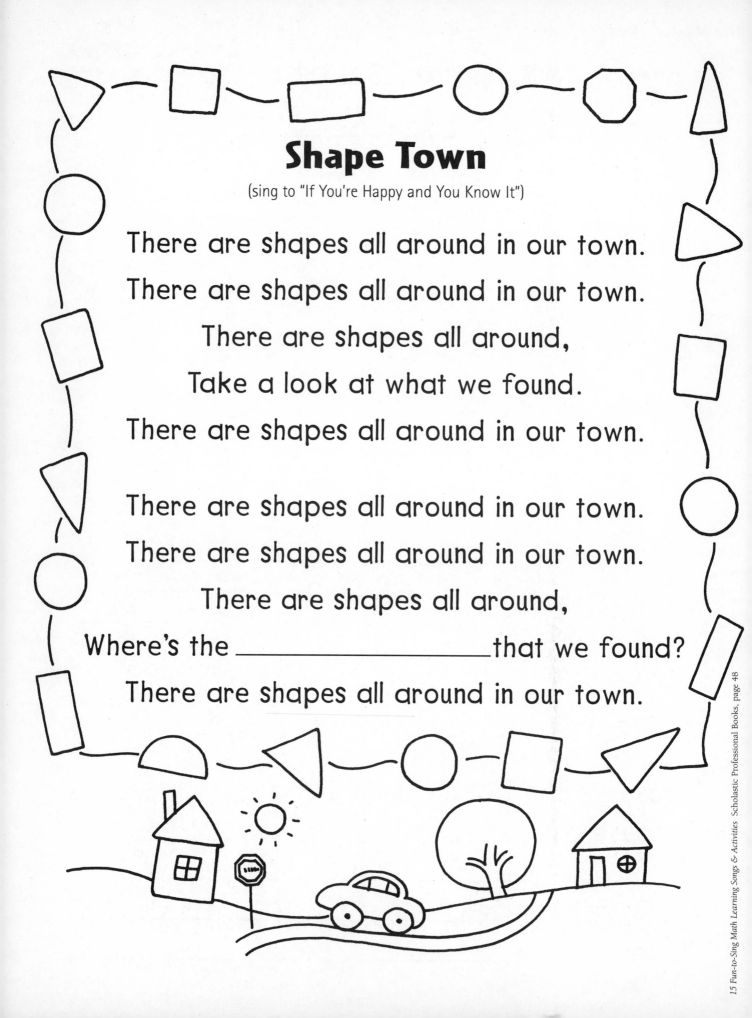

Shape Town

Children identify and record shapes.

SINGING THE SONG

Materials

* reproducible song sheet (page 48)
* traffic signs (from the block center or made from construction paper, one per child)
* self-sticking notes with shapes and shape words (circle, rectangle, square, triangle, diamond)
* blank chart paper

In advance, prepare song chart (see page 5 for tips).

1. Sing aloud as you track the words. Then sing again, inviting children to join in. Continue until children are familiar with the song.

2. Sing aloud while substituting the different self-sticking notes in the blank. Have children hold their sign up when its shape is mentioned.

3. Create a bar graph on chart paper to show how many children had each shape.

Materials

* 12- by 18-inch colored construction paper (one sheet per child)
* reproducible song sheet (one per child, page 48)
* recording sheet (one per child, page 51)
* crayons or markers

1. Have children each choose one of the shapes they sang about. Demonstrate how to write the name of the shape on the blank line of their song page, and have children cut out the song and glue it onto the construction paper.

2. Ask children: "How many more of these shapes can you find in our classroom?" Show children how to make tally marks on their recording sheet to record their discoveries.

3. Let children walk around the room, tallying their findings and completing the sheet. They can then glue their pages onto the construction paper and decorate the page with shapes. Bind all pages into a class book.

Assess

Take a shape walk around the school. Provide a recording sheet for children to identify circles, triangles, squares, rectangles, and so on with tally marks. Observe each child to see if he or she can accurately identify the different shapes.

Extend Learning

Social Studies and Math Invite children to build a shape town with building blocks. Provide paper shapes for children to glue onto paper to illustrate their shape town.

Technology Explore and identify 3-D solids on the software CD *Mighty Math Zoo Zillions* (Edmark Corporation and Harcourt Brace, 1997) with the "3D Gallery."

Book Links

Tana Hoban's *Circles, Triangles, and Squares* (Macmillan, 1974) and *I Read Signs* (Greenwillow, 1983) feature photos of shapes around the world.

Enjoy finding shapes in a colorful picture book, *Bear in a Square*, by Stella Blackstone (Scholastic, 1998).

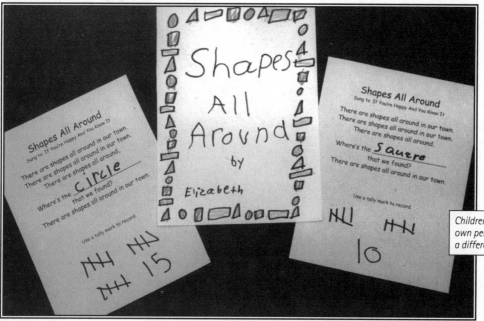

Children might also make their own personal shape books with a different shape for each page.

Name _____

I looked for _____ in our classroom.

This is what my shape looks like:

My Tally:

The most interesting _____ I found
in our classroom was _____ .

The Zoo

(sing to "Twinkle, Twinkle Little Star")

At _____ o'clock we went to the zoo

To see just what the animals do.

Right at _____ :30 we saw a giraffe

Playing with water and taking a bath.

Then at _____ o'clock we heard a roar

We ran to the lions and listened to more.

On to the monkeys to see them swing

At _____ :30 they began to sing.

Around _____ o'clock the kangaroos were out

Hopping around with their babies all about.

At _____ :30 it was time to go

We waved to the creatures and said thanks for the show.

The Zoo

Children will practice telling time to the hour and half hour.

SINGING THE SONG

Materials

* reproducible song sheet (page 52)
* large clock with movable hands
* self-sticking notes numbered 1 to 12

In advance, prepare song chart (see page 5 for tips).

1. Sing the song aloud as you track the words. Sing it again and invite children to sing along. Continue until children are familiar with the song.

2. Review telling time to the hour and half hour using a large clock, manipulating the hands of the clock as you do so.

3. Continue singing the song and changing the hour and half hour blanks, using self-sticking notes. Have a volunteer move the hands on the clock to indicate the times in each blank.

You might also use individual clocks with movable hands for each child.

Materials

* reproducible mini-book pages (one set per child, pages 55–58)
* pencil
* crayons or markers

1. Instruct children to fill in the hour and half hour blanks in their books and to complete each clock face to match the time written. They can use the times provided in the song or "start" their trip at any time they wish.

2. Have children illustrate each page, cut along the dotted lines, and then put the pages in order, stapling along the left edge to create their own mini-book.

Assess

Review each child's book and observe:
* Did the child record times in the blanks?
* Do the clock faces match the time recorded in the blanks?

Extend Learning

Math and Language Arts Create a schedule of the school day. Assign each child a different time of the day to write and illustrate, including a clock face indicating the time. Together, vote on and graph children's favorite time of the day.

Technology Use "Time Twins" on the software CD *Trudy's Time and Place House* (Edmark Corporation, 1995) to practice telling time on both digital and analog clocks by hour, half hour, and quarter hour.

Language Arts Use animals to create similes such as soft as a _____, or quiet as a _____.

Physical Education Create animal cards for children to pick from a hat. Instruct each child to act out the animal he or she chooses as others guess that animal.

Book Links

Visit the animals at a zoo with a little girl and her daddy in Mem Fox's *Zoo-Looking* (Mondo, 1996).

Spend the day with a young boy, and notice how time is measured in Bruce McMillan's *Time to...* (Scholastic, 1989).

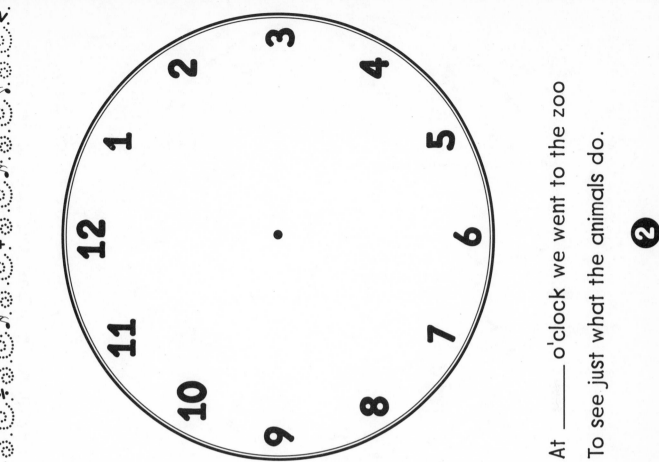

At _____ o'clock we went to the zoo

To see just what the animals do.

2

The Zoo

(sing to "Twinkle, Twinkle Little Star")

by _____

1

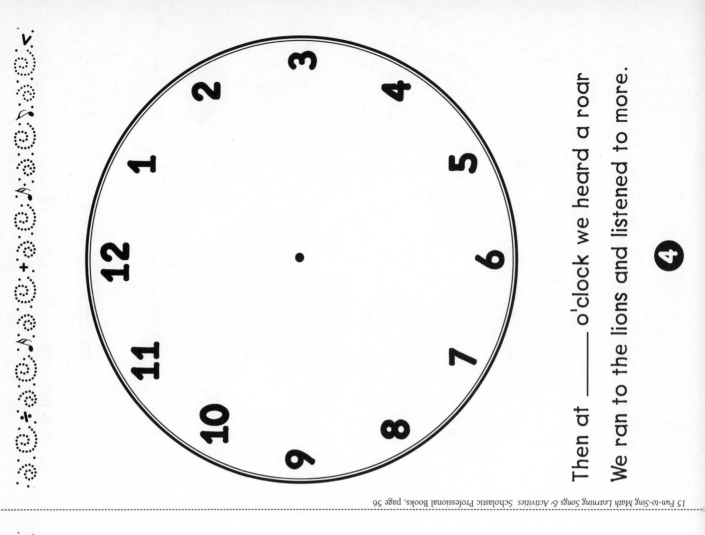

Then at _____ o'clock we heard a roar

We ran to the lions and listened to more.

4

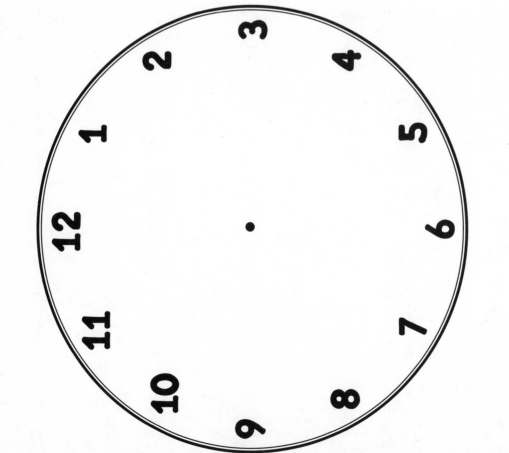

Right at _____ :30 we saw a giraffe

Playing with water and taking a bath.

3

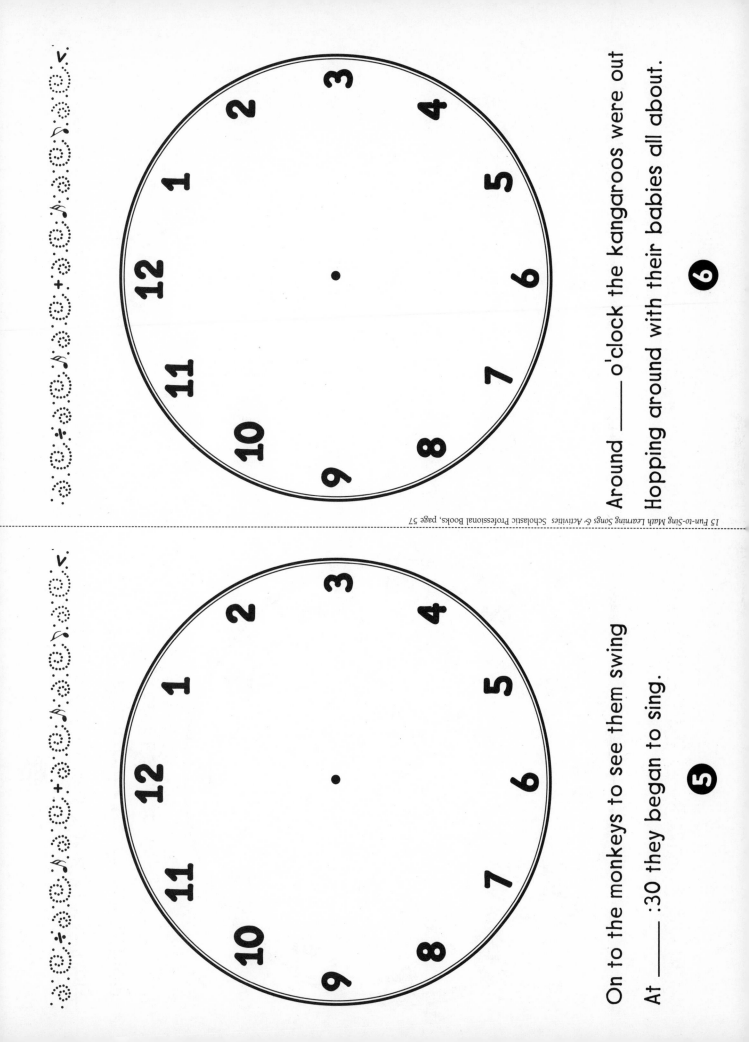

Around _____ o'clock the kangaroos were out

Hopping around with their babies all about.

6

On to the monkeys to see them swing

At _____ :30 they began to sing.

5

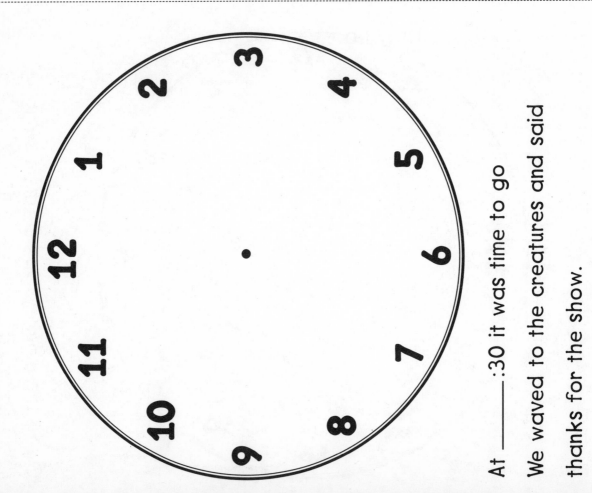

At _____ :30 it was time to go

We waved to the creatures and said

thanks for the show.

7

Under the Sea

(sing to "The Itsy Bitsy Spider")

On a fishing boat that goes out on the sea,

I took my pole to catch the fish all around me.

I caught a great big _____

that no one would believe.

So I measured just how long it was for everyone to see.

Under the Sea

Children will enjoy fishing for sea creatures to sing about and measure.

SINGING THE SONG

Materials

* reproducible song sheet (page 59)
* self-sticking notes with the name of a sea creature on each
* fishing pole (pencil with string tied to it and a small magnet tied to the end of the string)
* props (fishing hat, pail, and so on)
* large laminated sea creatures with paper clips attached to them (copy page 62 onto colored construction paper)

In advance, prepare song chart (see page 5 for tips).

1. Sing the song aloud as you track the words, and invite children to sing along. Continue until children are familiar with the song.

2. Have one child pretend to be in a fishing boat. He or she catches a sea creature with the pencil by hooking it onto the magnet. Fill in that sea creature's name in the blank in the song.

3. Together, measure the length of the sea creature using standard or nonstandard measurement. (You might use Unifix™ cubes or craft sticks to measure.)

4. Repeat, selecting a different sea creature to sing about and measure.

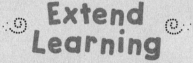

MAKING THE BOOK

Materials

- 12- by 18-inch sheets of blue construction paper
- reproducible song sheet (page 59)
- measuring page (one per child, page 63)
- pennies
- rulers
- crayons and markers
- scissors
- glue

1. Place the sea creatures in a center, and have children choose a sea animal to measure.

2. Have children fill in the blank on the song page, cut out the song, and glue it to the construction paper. Then have them measure the length of their creature as indicated on the measuring page, draw a picture of it, and glue that page to their paper.

3. Bind all pages together into a class book.

Children can use nonstandard measurement such as Unifix™ cubes, pennies, or their very own fingers to measure their creatures.

Assess

Compile all recording sheets completed by each child. While viewing the work, ask the child:
- Which sea creature was the longest?
- Which was the shortest?
- Were any the same in length?

Extend Learning

Language Arts Discuss homophones, using the example of sea/see from the song. List others: hear/here, peek/peak, two/to/too, some/sum, bear/bare, for/four.

Science Research an animal from the sea. Have children discover the actual size of the animal and then try to reproduce its size in chalk on the playground.

Technology *Math Keys: Unlocking Measurement K-2* (Houghton Mifflin and MECC, 1996) supports students as they complete measurement activities on the computer.

Book Links

Commotion in the Ocean, by Giles Andreae (Scholastic, 1998), is a collection of silly sea rhymes.

Measuring Penny, by Loreen Leedy (Henry Holt, 1997), demonstrates the many different ways to measure, including standard to nonstandard measurement, comparing weight, volume, time, temperature, and money.

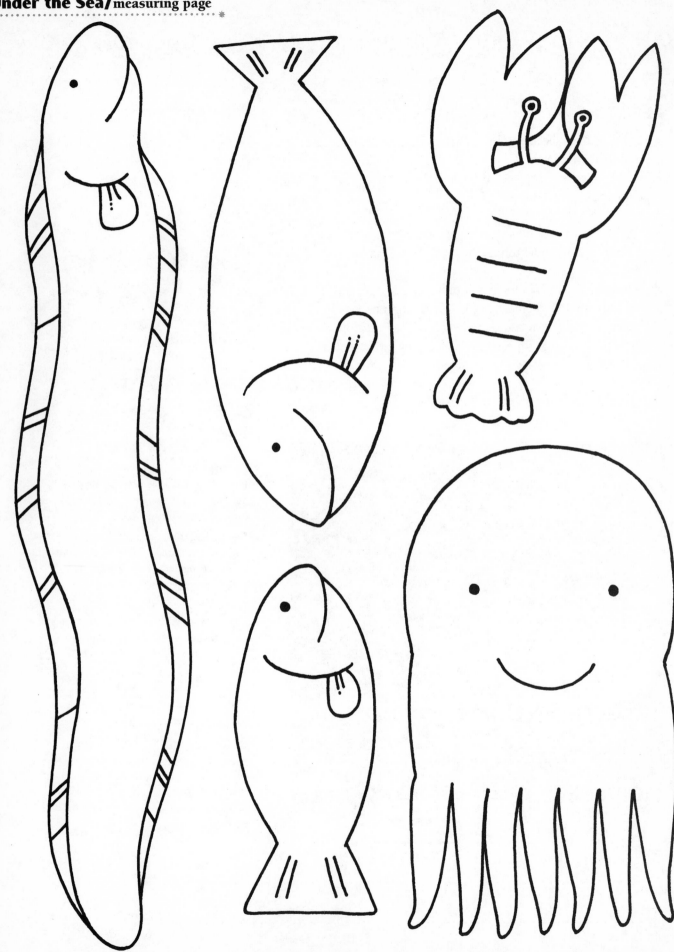

Name _____

I measured a _____.

I measured my _____ in:

inches: _____

pennies: _____

fingers: _____

_____ : _____

_____ : _____

The Piggy Bank

(sing to "Shortnin' Bread")

What's in my piggy bank, piggy bank, piggy bank?

What's in my piggy bank worth _____ cent(s)?

It's a shiny _____ , _____ , _____ .

It's a shiny _____ worth _____ cent(s)!

The Piggy Bank

Children practice identifying coins and make their very own individual piggy bank book.

SINGING THE SONG

Materials

* reproducible song sheet (page 64)
* 8 self-sticking notes (labeled: penny, nickel, dime, quarter, 1, 5, 10, and 25)
* coins or models of each coin (one per child, found in teacher supply stores)

In advance, prepare song chart (see page 5 for tips).

1. Sing the song aloud as you track the words. Sing it again and invite children to sing along. Continue until children are familiar with the song.

2. Present the various coins and review the coin names and their values. Distribute a different type of coin to each child.

3. Sing the song aloud, using self-sticking notes to fill in the blanks. When the song mentions a specific coin, children who have that coin should hold it up for others to see. Continue singing until each coin has been identified.

4. Repeat this activity, first having children trade coins. Depending on children's level, you might ask questions, such as "How many pennies do we have all together? If all the nickels and dimes were put together, how much would we have?"

Models of coins can be purchased in teacher supply stores.

MAKING THE BOOK

Materials

* piggy bank patterns (one per child, page 67, copied onto pink construction paper)
* reproducible mini-book pages (one set per child, pages 68-69)
* scissors
* glue
* crayons or markers
* pencil
* stapler

1. Have children cut out the piggy bank pattern for the cover of their book and write their name in the blank.

2. On each page of the mini-book, have children fill in the name of each coin and its value.

3. Children can cut along the dotted lines, put their pages in order and staple along the left edge to create a mini-book.

You might also cut out shapes for a realistic piggy bank.

Assess

Using children's individual booklets, observe:
* Does the child correctly identify the name and value of each coin?
* Has the child put the pages in order?
* Can the child read through his or her book independently?

Extend Learning

Math and Social Studies Investigate the possibility of Kids' Bank Days. Some banks have programs in which representatives visit schools so that children can make deposits into their very own savings accounts. To establish the account, a note is sent home explaining the program to parents, who sign a permission form and encourage their children to bring in a portion of their allowance for their savings account.

Art Create "rub over" booklets. Have each child use the side of a crayon and rub over a coin. Once the imprint appears on the paper, have children label the name of the coin and record its value.

Technology Learn about money with the "Gnu Ewe Boutique" on the software CD *Mighty Math Zoo Zillions* (Edmark Corporation and Harcourt Brace, 1997).

Book Links

The Purse, by Kathy Caple (Houghton Mifflin, 1986), is a delightful tale about saving money.

In Judith Viorst's *Alexander, Who Used to Be Rich Last Sunday* (Atheneum, 1978), readers learn about the woes of spending money.

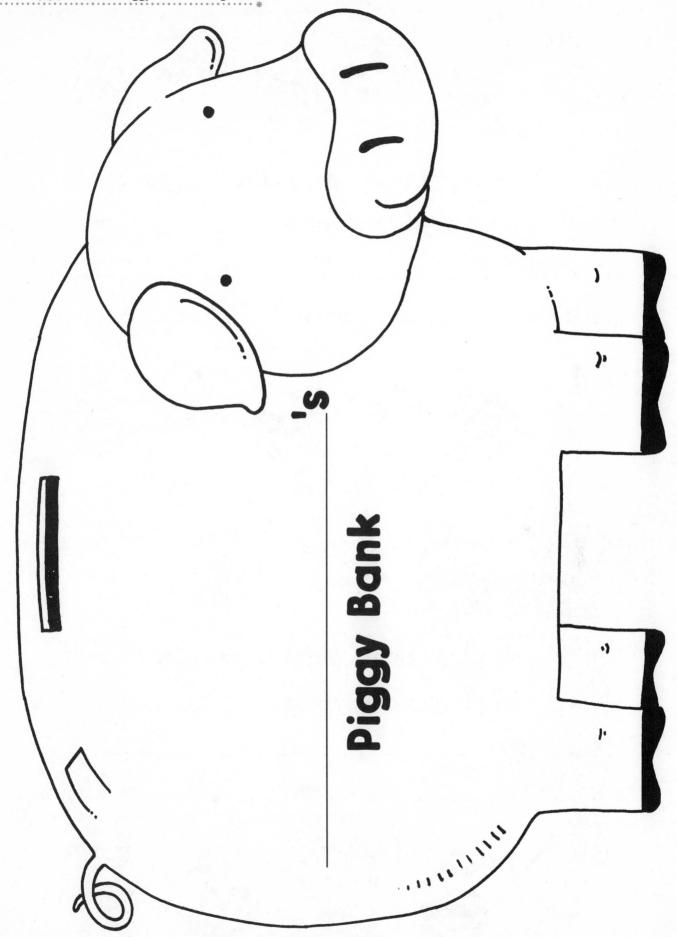

's

Piggy Bank

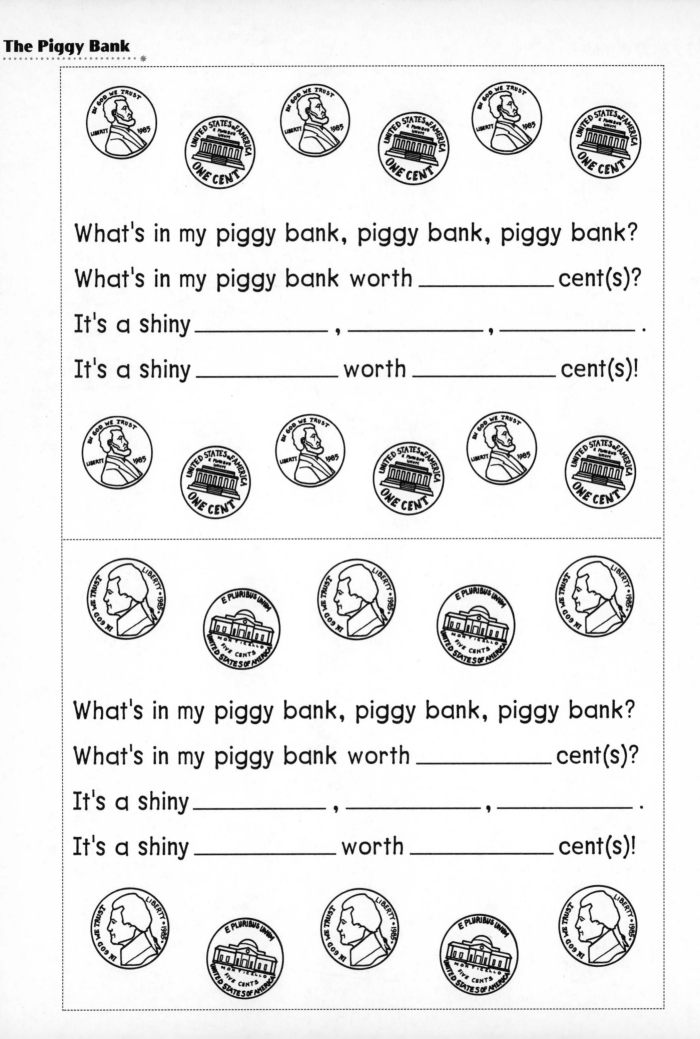

What's in my piggy bank, piggy bank, piggy bank?

What's in my piggy bank worth _____ cent(s)?

It's a shiny _____ , _____ , _____ .

It's a shiny _____ worth _____ cent(s)!

What's in my piggy bank, piggy bank, piggy bank?

What's in my piggy bank worth _____ cent(s)?

It's a shiny _____ , _____ , _____ .

It's a shiny _____ worth _____ cent(s)!

What's in my piggy bank, piggy bank, piggy bank?

What's in my piggy bank worth _____ cent(s)?

It's a shiny _____ , _____ , _____ .

It's a shiny _____ worth _____ cent(s)!

What's in my piggy bank, piggy bank, piggy bank?

What's in my piggy bank worth _____ cent(s)?

It's a shiny _____ , _____ , _____ .

It's a shiny _____ worth _____ cent(s)!

To the Grocery Story

(sing to "Three Blind Mice")

To the grocery store we go,

To the grocery store we go.

Because our food is low,

Because our food is low.

We'll get some food from the milk and the meats.

The veggies and fruits and the bread make nice treats.

Our bags will overflow,

Our bags will overflow.

To the Grocery Store

Children create a food graph.

SINGING THE SONG

Materials

* reproducible song sheet (page 70)
* pretend food
* large floor graph
* index cards with names of each food group

In advance, prepare song chart (see page 5 for tips).

1. Sing the song aloud as you track the words. Sing it again and invite children to join in. Continue until all children are familiar with the song.

2. Have children sit around the floor graph (put the index cards on the graph to indicate the different columns). Sing the song again and instruct children to put all foods from one food group, such as the dairy group, on the floor graph in the appropriate column.

3. Sing the song again and ask for foods from another food group. Continue until all food groups have been identified and children have put their foods in the appropriate columns.

4. Discuss the data that was collected. Encourage children to look at the graph and describe what they see. You might ask: "How many more foods are in the _____ group than the _____ group? Do any of the groups have the same number of foods? How many fewer foods are there in the _____ group than in the _____ group?"

For the floor graph, children might bring their favorite food from home or choose a favorite food from the pretend center or magazine pictures. You can also use a window shade and colored electrical tape for the lines on the graph; it rolls up easily for storage.

MAKING THE BOOK

Materials

* grocery graph (one per child, page 73)
* pencils and crayons

1. Guide children in completing the graph on the reproducible page.

2. Collect individual graphs and bind into a class book titled "Graphing Groceries."

To the Grocery Store

Name _____

Think of your five (or more!) favorite foods. Draw each one in the correct column. From which food group are most of your favorite foods? Circle that food group.

Fruit	Vegetables	Grains	Meat & Other Protein	Dairy

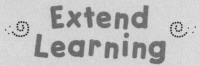

Assess

After making the individual graph, observe whether or not the child accurately created the graph. Looking at each child's work, ask them:

* Which column has the most foods?
* Which column has the fewest foods?
* Do any columns have the same number of foods?

Extend Learning

Science Using paper plates, instruct children to use the food groups to draw a balanced meal.

Technology Use the software program *The Graph Club* (Tom Snyder Productions, 1997) to help children gather, sort, and classify information. They can also construct graphs, analyze their data, and print graphs in multiple sizes.

Math Graph the same foods as before but use different attributes: like or dislike; small, medium, or large; color; and so on).

Book Links

Eating the Alphabet, by Lois Ehlert (Harcourt Brace, 1989), invites children to explore a delicious alphabet of fruit and vegetables.

Loreen Leedy's book *The Edible Pyramid* (The Holiday House, 1994) introduces the food pyramid to young readers as they discover good foods to eat.

15 Fun-to-Sing Math Learning Songs & Activities Scholastic Professional Books, page 73

Name _____

Think of your five (or more!) favorite foods. Draw each one in the correct column. From which food group are most of your favorite foods? Circle that food group.

Fruit	Vegetables	Grains	Meat & Other Protein	Dairy

Ladybug Spots, Ladybug Dots

(sing to "The Ants Go Marching")

Ladybugs have many spots. Hurrah! Hurrah!

Ladybugs have many spots. Hurrah! Hurrah!

Ladybugs have many spots.

Put _____ on its wings and touch the dots.

Count one by one!

There sure are lots!

Ladybug Spots, Ladybug Dots

Children play with spots and dots as they explore one-to-one correspondence.

SINGING THE SONG

Materials

* reproducible song sheet (page 74)
* large circle of red felt
* small black felt circles
* black felt strips ("legs")
* flannel board

* ladybug pattern (one per child, page 77, copied onto red construction paper)
* small black pompoms, black buttons, or black beans (one handful per child)

In advance, prepare song chart (see page 5 for tips) and create the ladybug felt prop by cutting a large piece of red felt into a round shape. Use black felt to create a head, antennae, legs, and circles for spots.

1. Sing aloud as you track the words. Sing it again and invite children to sing along. Continue with this until children are familiar with the song.

2. Using a felt board, the large felt ladybug, and black felt circles, model how to add spots on each side of the ladybug.

3. Distribute the ladybug patterns and the black pompoms to children. Instruct children to copy the number of spots from the felt ladybug.

4. Continue singing this song while changing the number blank until children demonstrate an understanding of this concept and correctly count the number of spots.

5. If time allows, have children work in pairs, singing the song while one child holds up a certain number of fingers and the other creates that number of spots on the ladybug workspace.

Materials

* ladybug pattern (one per child, page 77, copied onto 9- by 12-inch red construction paper)
* reproducible song sheet (one per child, page 74)
* 9- by 12-inch white construction paper
* scraps of black construction paper or black pipe cleaners
* scissors
* glue
* brad fasteners
* black crayons or markers

1. Have children cut out the reproducible song. Instruct them to fill in the number blank with a number of their choice.

2. Then have children cut out the red ladybug to be used for the cover. Demonstrate how to cut on the line that divides the circle in half, creating wings.

3. Attach the red wings to the top of the song using a brad fastener so that each red wing will open and close over the song page.

4. Invite children to draw spots on the red ladybug wings. The number of spots drawn should match the number written on the blank in their song.

5. Allow children to add more details with crayons and use either black construction paper or pipe cleaners to create the legs and antennae (these can be attached to the back side of the song sheet).

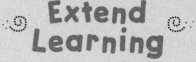

Assess

Review each child's ladybug and observe the following:
* Can the child accurately count the dots?
* Does the child touch each dot while saying the number aloud?
* Did the child accurately record the number?

Extend Learning

Math To teach the concept of doubling, one line of this song can be changed to say "Put _____ on one side and double the dots." Children then write a number sentence illustrating a double (for example, 2 + 2 = 4).

Science Discuss the characteristics of an insect (three body parts, two antennae, and six legs). Allow children to draw their own made-up insect.

Language Arts and Math Read *Domino Addition*, by Dr. Lynette Long (Scholastic, 1996), and allow children to identify the dominoes in the book. Follow up this book by providing dominoes to children so that they can practice counting and recording the numbers that appear on the dominoes.

Book Links

Ten Black Dots, by Donald Crews (Greenwillow, 1986), will engage children in counting.

Meet a grouchy ladybug in Eric Carle's *The Grouchy Ladybug* (Scholastic, 1977), as she travels meeting other creatures at different times during the day.

Ladybug Spots, Ladybug Dots/ladybug pattern

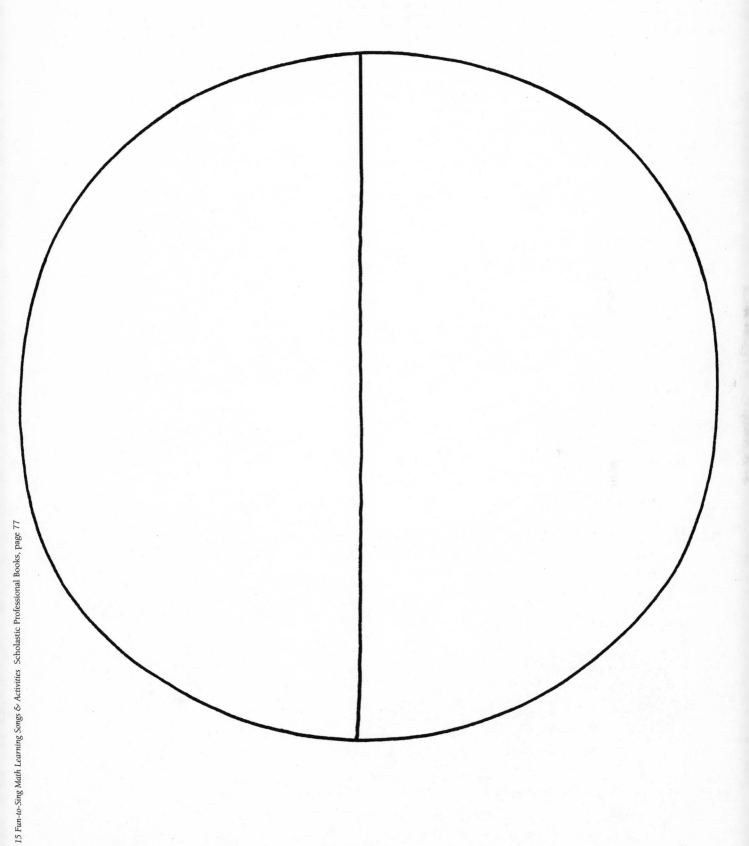

Notes

Notes

Notes